SETTLE TO CARLISLE

A BEAUTIFUL JOURNEY NORTH

SETTLE TO CARLISLE

A BEAUTIFUL JOURNEY NORTH

ANTHONY LAMBERT

SIENA

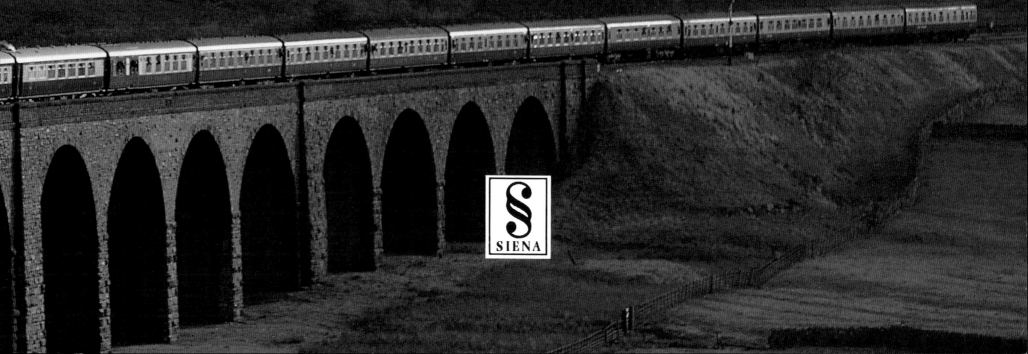

This is a Siena book

Siena is an imprint of Parragon

Parragon
13 Whiteladies Road
Clifton
Bristol BS8 1PB

ISBN: 0-75252-631-6

Conceived, designed and produced by Haldane Mason, London

Acknowledgements
Art Director: Ron Samuels
Editor: Charles Dixon-Spain
Designers: Errol Campbell/Zoë Mellors
Illustrator: Claire Littlejohn
Indexer: Ian D. Crane
Picture Research: Charles Dixon-Spain

Colour reproduction by
Regent Publishing Services, Hong Kong

Printed in Italy

Picture Acknowledgements
Ken Groundwater 17 (left), 22; **Hulton Picture Library** 64; **Gavin W. Morrison** 2, 5, 11, 17 (right), 18, 19, 21, 23, 28, 35, 43, 46, 48, 49 (bttm), 52, 53, 54, 60, 68, 75, 80, 81, 83, 93; **National Railway Museum, York (Science & Society Picture Library)** 8, 9 (left), 12, 14, 16, 24, 25, 26 (all), 31, 33, 34; **Dr. Les Nixon** 1, 9 (right), 27, 30, 32, 36, 42, 44, 51, 55, 58, 59, 62, 63, 65, 66, 69, 70, 74, 81 (bttm), 82, 85, 87, 88, 94; **Railfoto/Hugh Ballantyne** 15, 40, 50, 72, 73, 80, 92; **Peter J. Robinson** 29, 32, 41, 76, 89, 91; **David C. Rodgers** 7, 38, 41, 45, 56, 61, 77, 78, 84.

Every effort has been made to trace the copyright holders and we apologize in advance for any unintentional errors or omissions. We would be pleased to insert the appropriate acknowledgement in any subsequent edition of this publication.

Please note: Stations currently in use are given in **bold** when first mentioned in the text.

Page 1: *Northbound excursion, pulled by K1 class No. 2005, labours up the Long Drag near Selside.*
Page 2/3: *Crossing Dandry Mire with the Duchess of Hamilton.*

Contents

INTRODUCTION 6

THE MIDLAND RAILWAY 8

ORIGINS 10

CONSTRUCTION 14

ARCHITECTURE 22

PASSENGER SERVICES 24

GOODS SERVICES 28

LOCOMOTIVES 30

OPERATION 33

SALVATION AND RENAISSANCE 35

MAP OF THE SETTLE & CARLISLE LINE 37

LEEDS–RIBBLEHEAD 38

RIBBLEHEAD–GARSDALE 46

GARSDALE–KIRKBY STEPHEN 56

KIRKBY STEPHEN–APPLEBY 70

APPLEBY–CARLISLE 78

INDEX 96

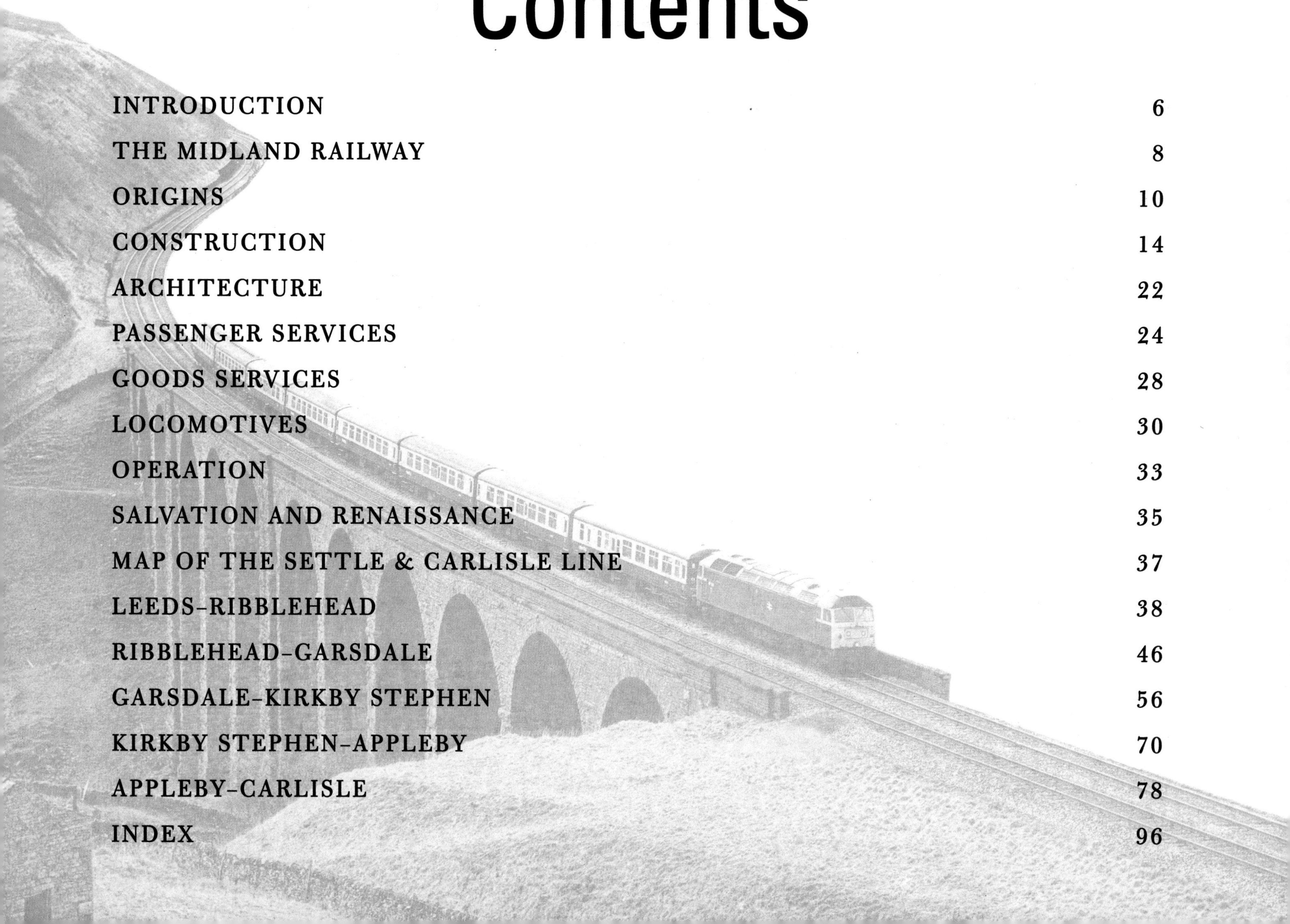

Introduction

No railway line in England has so captured the public imagination as the Settle & Carlisle railway (otherwise known as the S&C). It was well known before the closure threat of the 1980s and the effective campaign to save it, but the publicity these generated made the 72^1/$_2$ mile route the subject of national news. The ironic result has been that more passengers use the railway today than at almost any time in its history. The reasons are obvious: the story of its genesis and construction encapsulates many of the most absurd and heroic themes of Victorian railway history, and the landscapes through which it passes are simply unrivalled for beauty and sheer grandeur by any other line in the country.

Almost from the first mile of the S&C line, which begins at Settle Junction, the railway is in the Yorkshire Dales National Park and remains so for about the first 25 miles. Climbing relentlessly through Ribblesdale and skirting the upper reaches of Dentdale and Garsdale to reach what passes for a plateau in this country, between Blea Moor and Ais Gill, the line drops down the Eden Valley to reach the great railway junction of Carlisle. It passes through landscapes that hold the eye of the most blasé traveller, and could equally well have been promoted by the advertising slogan that British Rail applied to the West Highland railway in Scotland – 'A line for all seasons'. It is the kind of railway that should be experienced at different times of the year, the quality of light in such landscapes changing dramatically their atmosphere. Between Horton-in-Ribblesdale and Kirkby Stephen, Yorkshire's 'Three Peaks' – Ingleborough, Penyghent and Whernside – are in view, giving to the railway a scale that is enjoyed by few railways in Britain. As early as 1908, when marketing was still in its infancy, the Midland tried to attract hikers to the S&C and put up Ordnance Survey maps in the stations.

Yet this magnificent stretch of railway should never have been built. The story behind its construction is involved but fascinating, since it illustrates well the mentality of Parliamentarians in their dealings with railways, and the unfortunate consequences that could ensue. But before looking at the origins of the Settle & Carlisle, it is necessary to look at the great railway company that brought it into being, the Midland.

Opposite: For generations, photographers of the S&C have regarded the landscape around Ais Gill as one of the best places to record the final slog up to the summit from either direction, but particularly trains from the north, enabling the dramatic outline of Wild Boar Fell to form a backdrop. Here LNER A3 Pacific No. 4472 Flying Scotsman struggles up the last stretch to the 356 m (1,169 ft) summit with a return special to Preston on 16 May 1992.

The Midland Railway

The Midland became a splendid railway, but its origins were local and modest. One of its constituents, the Midland Counties, was founded at a meeting of local coal-owners in a pub in Eastwood, round a few corners from D.H. Lawrence's birthplace. Goods traffic, and especially coal, was the raison d'être.

The Midland was incorporated in 1844 by the amalgamation of three companies that operated in the Midlands area – the Midland Counties, the North Midland and the Birmingham & Derby Junction. Masterminded by George Hudson, whose 'Railway King' epithet belied the sharp practice that proved his eventual downfall, the merger produced the largest railway under single management in Britain.

The subsequent history of the Midland is dominated by its struggle to become a national, rather than regional, railway. This was achieved by a combination of takeovers and construction. For example, it reached Bristol by taking over the Birmingham & Gloucester and the Bristol & Gloucester railways in 1846. By building new lines it gained access to such cities as Lincoln and Peterborough in 1846, Manchester in 1867 and London in 1868, the last entailing construction of the costly line from Bedford to St. Pancras with its magnificent train shed, station and hotel. The Midland became particularly adept at forming alliances with other companies, often formalized in joint ownership of a section of railway. Amongst the more important of its arrangements, it became a partner in the Cheshire Lines Committee, thereby reaching Liverpool; the Somerset & Dorset to reach Bournemouth; and the Midland & Great Northern to tap the holiday traffic to the north Norfolk resorts and East Anglia generally. The Midland had a stake in Scotland, being a partner in the Portpatrick & Wigtownshire Joint Railways and in the company that built the Forth Bridge. It even reached the Atlantic by the acquisition of two railways in Ireland in 1903 and 1905. Finally it acquired a major slice of the London commuter traffic through its purchase of the London, Tilbury & Southend Railway in 1912. So from its early days, the Midland had ambitious goals.

In this, it was no different from other entrepreneurial railway managements of the time, but it was much more successful than most. Having risen in only a couple of decades from meetings in the back rooms of pubs to become some of the largest joint-stock enterprises anywhere in the world, the Midland, like the other larger railway companies, had an understandable optimism and belief in its ability to overcome difficulties. As Alexander Frater wrote of the two men who did most to being the S&C into being, 'Allport and Crossley were messianic Victorian visionaries who, having voted God on to the Midland board years before, felt able to tackle the trickiest problems with equilibrium.'

George Hudson was the architect behind the formation of the Midland Railway, before his dubious business practices led to his ignominious downfall.

The Midland had also become a railway of quality: its resources and profitability enabled it to construct well-designed stations using good materials, and it was renowned for the standard of upholstery and finish of its carriages. The Midland's development of comfort in its carriages placed it in the vanguard of British railway companies, especially in its concern for third-class passengers. As the Midland's great General Manager Sir James Allport said as he neared retirement, 'If there is one part of my public life on which I look back with more satisfaction than on anything else, it is with reference to the boon we conferred on third-class passengers.' However, the adoption of the beautiful crimson lake livery known as 'Midland red' with which it adorned both locomotives and carriages from 1883 was the result of an attempt to find a less fugitive and economic colour than the previous green livery for locomotives.

The characteristics evident from this resumé – determination, national aspirations and a commitment to quality – were brought to bear on one of the major difficulties that faced the Midland in the 1860s, the unacceptable delays to which its Scottish traffic was subjected.

Right: The Gothic Midland Hotel at St. Pancras, designed by Sir Gilbert Scott, has become one of London's most valued landmarks, appropriately listed Grade I. Below: William Barlow's magnificent train shed at St. Pancras has the highest arched roof of any station in Europe.

Origins

The Midland had already grown tired of an irksome dependence on other railways for forwarding its traffic to major destinations. Until the opening of a new line from Leicester to Hitchin in 1857, the Midland had relied on the London & North Western Railway (LNWR) for its London traffic, which it handed over at Rugby. Overcrowding on the West Coast main line inevitably meant that the LNWR was given priority. From the opening of the railway to Hitchin, the Midland transferred London traffic to the Great Northern Railway (GNR) which owned the railway into King's Cross. It also marked a change in allegiances for the Midland, ending its southern reliance on the LNWR and forging a closer link with the GNR.

The introduction of through Midland services into King's Cross in 1858 was a short-lived improvement; by 1862 the situation between Hitchin and King's Cross was so bad that 3,400 Midland trains were delayed that year, and in June and July the congestion had reduced both companies' traffic to chaos. The Midland determined on its own line into London. The treatment of the Midland's traffic with Scotland was little different. It was again dependent on the LNWR, handing over passengers and goods traffic at an obscure end-on junction named Ingleton. This arrangement had existed since 1861, when the Lancaster & Carlisle Railway (LCR) opened its line to Ingleton from a junction with the West Coast main line at Low Gill. The Lancaster & Carlisle directors had secured in 1859 very favourable terms for a 999-year lease to the LNWR. So the Midland was again beholden to the LNWR, which did little to smooth the operation of the Midland's traffic: stories of long waits for connections at Tebay and goods traffic taking an age to reach Carlisle fuelled the Midland's desire for a route of its own to Scotland, and it began to talk of the idea.

Because of the onerous terms of its lease of the LCR, and doubtless worried at the thought of a third main line to Scotland, the LNWR proposed in 1864 the idea of a joint lease of the LCR with the Midland. This would have given an equal voice in the handling of traffic over the line, and overcome the Midland's objections to the current position. Had these negotiations succeeded, the S&C would probably not have been built, but they foundered over the LNWR's insistence that it should have the power to regulate Midland rates on traffic to Carlisle. A less insuperable stumbling block was the LNWR's proposal that the LCR rent should be split equally between the two; this would have been very much in the LNWR's favour, since it would probably have had a much heavier traffic over the route than would ever have been built up by the Midland.

Meanwhile, north of the border, a new railway had been built that would have a bearing on the S&C. In the summer of 1862, the North British Railway completed its Waverley route from Edinburgh to Carlisle; since it was in competition with the Caledonian Railway (CR), which had a very close relationship with the LNWR, the North British was always playing second fiddle when it came to connections at Carlisle. Consequently it welcomed the prospect of a new main line from the south and a partnership with its operator.

In 1865 a Bill was put before Parliament that the Midland was to modify and re-present in the following year as the Bill for the S&C. The North of England Union Railway was for a line from a junction with the Skipton–Lancaster line south of Settle to Hawes and along Wensleydale to Leyburn on the North Eastern Railway. Without Midland intervention it would have died the death of so many hopelessly unrealistic schemes hatched in one of the two 'Railway Manias'. Such a line would never have attracted enough local traffic to make a commercial return, but the Midland saw it as an ideal vehicle for its main line to Scotland.

In August 1865 John Crossley, the Midland's Engineer, was instructed to survey the route. The possibility of North Eastern Railway opposition was nullified by the Midland truncating its eastern aspirations at Hawes. However, some Midland shareholders were not in favour of the expenditure of an estimated £1.65 million on the new line, and said so at meetings. One prescient shareholder suggested that the cost would be nearer £3 million; had his

Opposite: One of the rebuilt Royal Scot 4-6-0s allocated to Leeds Holbeck for Anglo-Scottish expresses, No. 46113 Cameronia prepares to leave the shed on 27 June 1961 to work the down 'Waverley'. The locomotive was built in 1927, rebuilt in May 1949 and withdrawn in December 1962.

warning been taken seriously, it is unlikely that shareholders would have voted for the S&C.

During the summer of 1866 a House of Commons committee heard evidence on the Midland Railway (Settle to Carlisle) Bill. Business interests from Carlisle told tales of woe about the difficulty of sending traffic through Ingleton to destinations in the Midlands, and support was given by the Glasgow & South Western, North British and Lancashire & Yorkshire railways, all frustrated in some degree by the LNWR's handling of their traffic at Carlisle or over the West Coast line. The Commons and Lords committees found in the Midland's favour and the Bill was given the Royal Assent on 16 July 1866, allowing five years for the railway's construction.

Although preparatory work for construction was begun by Crossley, it was to be three years before the Midland really had the bit between its teeth. Firstly, a reduction in the Midland dividend did not dispose shareholders favourably either to a proposed amalgamation with the Glasgow & South Western Railway or the amount of money that the Midland was

Surmounted by the Wyvern of Mercia, the heraldic device of the Midland included the arms of Bristol, Derby, Leeds, Leicester and Lincoln, supported by a dolphin and a salamander.

needs over the LCR and so more formal talks between the Midland and the LNWR were held in July and August of 1868 to see if some accommodation could be reached.

Negotiations were sufficiently favourable for the Midland directors to consider dropping the S&C, but they faced a dilemma. To cancel the S&C an abandonment Bill would have to be put before Parliament, but the outcome would not be known until May 1869. On the other hand, two years of the S&C Bill had already elapsed without any material work having been done, and on 16 July 1869 the Midland's powers for the compulsory purchase of land would lapse, necessitating an extension of powers. How could the Midland apply for a Bill to abandon the S&C at the same time as it sought an extension of powers to build it?

The only course was to put the quandary openly before the LNWR board, which could see that the Midland had little option but to present both Bills. By November 1868 agreement between the two railways for the Midland's use of the LCR had been reached,

committed to laying out on a range of new works – estimated at £5 million. The two issues became bound up, and a group of Midland shareholders approached the LNWR to try to negotiate a new agreement for use of the LCR. Those trying to stop the S&C proceeding were fearful of the impact the costs would have on their dividends – and perhaps on those of the LNWR, since many held shares in both companies. In the event, the Lords rejected the amalgamation Bill.

The deteriorating economic position in the country at large towards the end of 1867 prompted the Midland board to suspend further work and land purchase for the S&C. The tide of opposition from shareholders was such that the Midland board felt it had no option but to agree to cooperate with a committee of consultation to look at ways of reducing or limiting the impact of outstanding new works. A dialogue between the committee and the LNWR suggested that the prospect of the S&C had concentrated the mind of the North Western board at Euston: much more conciliatory ideas were put forward to meet the Midland's

and the LNWR would support the S&C abandonment Bill.

The alliances that had debated the merits of the original S&C Bill were now turned on their heads. The Midland's erstwhile supporters now became staunch opponents of the abandonment Bill. The pros and cons of cancelling the S&C were closely argued before a House of Commons committee in April 1869, and it is hard to find fault with the arguments put forward by the Midland's counsel, but the opposition mounted a strong case that their traffic would not be helped by joint working of the LCR in the way that it would by construction of the S&C. The fervent determination of Parliament to do all in its power to resist anything that smacked of monopoly status, and to stimulate competition irrespective of possible waste, informed many of the decisions it took about railways in the Victorian era. And so it was with the S&C abandonment Bill. After seven days of hearings, the committee found the preamble of the Bill not proven. The Midland was committed to building the S&C.

LMS Jubilee class 4-6-0 No. 45562 Alberta heads the up (southbound) Waverley at Ais Gill in about 1960. These were the last express engines to operate the S&C in BR days.

Construction

The sheer scale of the task facing the engineer charged with building the S&C, John Sidney Crossley, must have been daunting, even for a man of his experience. It is a pity that there is no diary of the epic walk that Crossley and Sir James Allport made of the route when the idea of the S&C was still in its infancy; it would be fascinating to know the impressions of the two men as they tramped across 'that terrible place, Blea Moor', as Sir James later recounted.

Although there were no complex bridges to build, such as those over the Tamar estuary at Saltash or across the Menai Strait, the number of structures was formidable: 85 overbridges, 150 underbridges, 25 viaducts with 168 openings and 13 tunnels. As a farmer said, with pardonable exaggeration, to the two pioneers during their walk: 'I declare to you there is not a level piece of ground big enough to build a house upon all the way between Settle and Carlisle.' Moreover the terrain was harsh and almost certain to provide some unpleasant surprises, which proved to be the case, compelling more costly and time-consuming solutions where no problem had been anticipated: embankments turned into viaducts, cuttings into tunnels.

Right: The imposing profile of Ribblehead Viaduct with a Carlisle-bound train.
Below: The arches of Ribblehead Viaduct, which required extensive work in the 1990s to remedy the effects of water working into the stonework and then freezing.

J. C. Bourne's depiction of Kilsby Tunnel on the London & Birmingham line shows the sort of desperate conditions the navvies of the S&C worked in.

The scale of the works was a reflection of the Midland's determination to produce a line for the express speeds of the day. By stipulating a maximum gradient of 1 in 100, the Midland denied itself the freedom to take full advantage of the contours of the hills as the North of England Union Railway (NEUR) had done in its plans for a railway from Settle to Hawes. When the Midland took over the project, it had to discard most of the route surveyed, since the NEUR was never intended to be more than a relatively slow, branch line. To maintain the capability of high speed running, the Midland was forced into much heavier engineering works. A by-product of the priority given to through, rather than intermediate traffic, is the distance that separates most of the stations from the towns or villages they were built to serve. The S&C was also constructed with little thought of economy in the engineering and architectural standards that were set; there was never a sense that the Midland was going to skimp on this railway simply because it had been forced into building it against its will.

In as much as it can be said that a railway was principally the work of one man, the S&C owed more to Crossley than anyone else. Crossley was the Midland's Engineer from 1857 to 1878. Orphaned at the age of two in 1815, he had clearly shown early promise, becoming engineer of the Leicester Navigation Canal at the age of 20. He first became involved with what became a constituent part of the Midland in 1832 when he carried out surveying work on the Leicester & Swannington Railway. The rest of his life was spent surveying and supervising the construction of hundreds of miles of the Midland, culminating with the S&C.

The line was scheduled for completion in just under four years, ready for opening in the summer of 1873. In fact it was another two years before the first goods train traversed the line and the opening to passengers did not take place until 1 May 1876. The works were divided into four contracts: No. 1, 17 miles from Settle Junction to Dent Head; No. 2, 17 miles on to Smardale; No. 3 14$^{1}/_{2}$ miles to New Biggin; and No. 4, the remaining 24 miles to Petteril Bridge.

Construction began in November 1869 with that very Victorian occasion, the cutting of the first sod, in the grounds of Anley House near Settle. Such events were usually attended by local worthies, as well as officials, and carried out with a ceremonial silver spade and beautifully crafted wheelbarrow.

Naturally a start was made on those works that were expected to take the longest; by March 1870 the shafts for Blea Moor Tunnel were well under way,

Though rudimentary, the facilities of a gangers' hut on the S&C would have been very welcome in winter, when the efficient stove could create quite a heat.

The plaque in the church at Settle which commemorates those killed and injured during construction of the S&C. The plaque was paid for by the MR and navvies.

and a number of boreholes sunk to determine the location of rock for viaduct foundations. However, it was quickly evident that work on No. 1 contract was slipping behind schedule, a position that was to worsen: the contractor had to ask the Midland for a loan, which it provided, but by October 1871 things had reached the point at which the Midland felt compelled to cancel the contract and assume direct responsibility for the work. This added significantly to the burden on Crossley. Finding enough navvies to progress the works at an adequate pace was another perennial problem. The appalling weather and

physical conditions ate away at the men's morale, and all but the most determined quit after months rather than years; on No. 2 contract there was a 73% turnover of navvies in a single month. Although there were up to 7,000 navvies at work at any one time, hundreds of thousands of men experienced the hardships of an S&C navvy's life. In common with most railway construction, navvies were lured away during harvest time, especially in the Eden Valley area, where their help in the fields was most needed. Rates of pay were good for the times. They had to be to attract men to work in such atrocious conditions, but many men

Above: LMS 4F 0-6-0 No. 44276 with large snowplough at Skipton shed in 1965.
Opposite: LNER A3 Pacific No. 4472 Flying Scotsman nears Ais Gill summit.

who were on piece rates decided that by about 15.00 they had earned enough for the day and downed tools. Those who were paid by the day put in the required number of hours but, as Crossley euphemistically put it, 'do not work to hurt themselves.'

Another difficulty was the transport of equipment, materials and supplies to such a remote area, in which there were few roads, and most were little more than farm tracks or drove roads. The component parts of stationary steam winding engines for the top of tunnel shafts had to be manhandled across boggy ground and up steep slopes. Once in place they had to be assembled in the open, with minimal facilities, and were then used to haul further supplies up the slopes. In contrast to railway construction a few decades earlier, the S&C was able to benefit from improved mechanisation in such equipment as drills and from safer materials, particularly dynamite rather than gun-cotton.

However, pick and shovel were still to the fore; by the time the Great Central main line to London came to be built in the final decade of the century, mechanical excavators were doing most of the work.

Nor were the soil conditions conducive to easy work. For much of the southern section the builders had to contend with boulder clay, which could change its nature from one day to the next. As Crossley recounted to the early historian of the Midland, Frederick Williams, 'I have known the men blast the boulder-clay like rock, and within a few hours to have to ladle out the same stuff from the same spot like soup in buckets. Or a man strikes a blow with his pick at what he thinks is clay, but there is a great boulder underneath almost as hard as iron, and the man's wrists, arms, and body are so shaken by the shock, that, disgusted, he flings down his tools, asks for his money, and is off.'

Conditions were inevitably worsened by the amount of rain that can lash the Dales, turning already difficult ground into quagmires. No. 2 contract was particularly affected by rain: cartwheels had to be replaced by massive rollers to prevent them sinking into the glutinous mud that the clay had become, horses sank up to their bellies and even dragging a telegraph pole along might require the exertions of four horses. Crossley was tried by some exceptionally bad weather: in 1872, for example, 152 cm (60 in) of rain fell at Kirkby Stephen instead of the average 94 cm (37 in).

Rain was not the only trial. Frost would halt masonry work for days and turn previously sticky clay as hard as concrete. Only the tunnellers could remain at work in such conditions: hundreds of feet below the surface of the moor, navvies laboured for 12-hour shifts in a stygian gloom, relieved only by the feeble light of candles. Williams went through the workings and thought them 'a picture fit for Rembrandt', though Wright of Derby might have been a more apposite choice.

Crossley had underestimated the impact the weather would have on the progress of the works. His reports to the Midland construction committee are full of frustration at the way inclement conditions not only impeded work, but encouraged those navvies on piece rates to leave altogether because they could not work enough hours to amass a decent wage.

Another factor which deterred navvies from staying long on the S&C was the high incidence of deaths and injuries: of those based at Batty Moss camp near Ribblehead alone, about a hundred died from all causes during construction. There was also the fear of smallpox – a severe outbreak at Ribblehead in 1871 was the principal cause behind the need to expand the graveyard at nearby Chapel-le-Dale, and it also broke out in Settle in 1871–2, prompting the Midland to give £100 to the town's smallpox hospital. Fighting, which was a way of life in the camps, caused a number of fatalities. On Sundays, when no work was done, bare-knuckle fights would be held for the title of camp champion, who might be pitted against a professional fighter brought in for the spectacle.

Though the navvies were undoubtedly rough and sometimes violent, there was another side to their behaviour. When the missionary for the 17 miles between Settle and Denthead, James Tiplady, left after two years' work in 1872, he was given a silver cruet and an illuminated address by the inhabitants of the camp at Ribblehead in appreciation of his efforts. He had described his flock as being 'with few exceptions a good-hearted, generously disposed class. The greatest enemy I have to contend with is strong drink. If this could be removed, a great boon would be conferred, not only upon the Missionary, but upon all who have anything to do with railway work.'

Goods trains began operating over the line in early August 1875 (there is some doubt over the precise date), and it opened to passenger trains without fuss or ceremony on 1 May 1876. The previous month the construction committee had toured the line in a cattle truck fitted out with wooden benches so that the party could enjoy a clear view. The combination of this unusual mode of travel with the grandeur of the landscapes induced an extravagant description from the *Sheffield & Rotherham Independent* reporter: 'There, in appropriate wrappings and in close-fitting caps, with nothing to obstruct their view of the line – they were enabled to appreciate the glories of land and sky, the ranges of mighty mountains, intersected by wild gorges or divided by lovely valleys. . . .' The correspondent went on to suggest that such vehicles might become a permanent option for hardier travellers, an idea that was certainly adopted in Switzerland and the United States.

In common with most civil engineering works on such a scale, the costs were underestimated: the line cost £3.8 million rather than the anticipated £2.2 million. Crossley cannot be blamed for much of the overspend. It was his and the Midland's misfortune that construction of the S&C should coincide with a period of exceptional inflation. The various causes behind several years of increases in prices and wages included, in 1866, the second Railway Mania and the collapse of the discount house Overend, Gurney & Co (which caused the worst panic in the city since 1825) and the Franco-Prussian War of 1870–1. The consequence was increases in some wages of up to 100 % within a year and a tripling in the price of coal between 1870 and 1876.

Class 47 No. 47104 crosses Arten Gill Viaduct with a Cleethorpes–Carlisle special. In recent years locomotives have been seen only on freight and diversions.

20

Architecture

Most of the station buildings on the S&C were based on a standard design evolved by Crossley which has been called 'Midland Gothic', though the architect of the S&C buildings was I. H. Sanders.

There were three levels of provision according to the anticipated traffic. A common feature of the two smaller categories was a central section housing a waiting area protected by a wood- or iron-framed screen, flanked by two gabled pavilions. The more important stations of Appleby and Settle had three pavilions, and Garsdale, Crosby Garrett and Culgaith had differently designed buildings. Many of the stations had low platforms, requiring portable wooden steps to assist some passengers.

Goods sheds were as solidly built as the stations, their size naturally determined by the expectations for traffic, ranging from a two-wagon shed at Armathwaite to five-wagon sheds at Settle, Kirkby Stephen and Appleby.

Materials were extracted locally to reduce transport costs, limestone being used in upper Ribblesdale, gritstone at Dent and Garsdale, and sandstone through the Eden Valley.

A measure of the railway's architectural and historic importance was the decision in 1991 by North Yorkshire County Council to designate the whole line within the Yorkshire Dales National Park as a conservation area. This includes lineside structures, the land on which Batty Moss shanty town once stood and even the heaps of spoil excavated from Blea Moor Tunnel. It is believed to be the first time that a working railway has been declared a linear conservation area.

The Friends of the Settle–Carlisle Line have also done much to retain the surviving buildings that lend such character to a journey over the line.

Right: Some of the decorative spandrels of the station roof at Hellifield are adorned with the Midland wyvern. For years under threat of demolition, the station has been given a new lease of life thanks to the imaginative co-operation of a range of organizations.
Opposite: Hellifield, like many a country junction, has lost its importance, but it may become a junction again if services from Blackburn are extended north.

Kirkby Stephen–Appleby

*The station at **Kirkby Stephen** is situated on a hill a mile above the linear market town built on the west bank of the River Eden. On the route of Wainwright's Coast-to-Coast walk, Kirkby Stephen was once served by an east–west railway running from Darlington to Tebay and to Penrith, which had been opened in the 1860s and closed in 1962. Part of the North Eastern Railway (NER), the railway was notable for its dramatically sited viaducts of tapering ironwork – there has even been a suggestion that lottery money might be used to reconstruct one.*

The NER station was closer to the town centre and retained a good share of the district's agricultural traffic, to the Midland's chagrin. The size of the goods shed and three-gabled station is indicative of the company's largely unfulfilled expectations.

Kirkby Stephen market is held on Monday in a square that was once host to the dubious pastime of bull-baiting; the area is marked by a ring of cobblestones, but the practice was stopped after 1820 when a bull broke free. Probably the busiest day of the year is the October Luke Fair, a cattle and sheep sale that generated heavy traffic for the railway. Local boys would hire themselves out on droving duties for the day, raising money to buy fireworks. In moving animals between the market and the two stations, inquisitive cows were known to enter houses whose owners had thoughtlessly left the front door open, with odiferous results.

The cloisters between the market square and the church were put up for shelter as a philanthropic gesture by a navy purser named John Waller who was born in the town. The oldest parts of the much-rebuilt church, which is shared by Anglicans and Catholics, date from the early thirteenth century. The nave of the parish church dates from 1220, the tower from around 1500. Unusually the church is not dedicated to any saint, and its great treasure is an eighth-century representation of Loki, the Norse god of strife and spirit of evil; in accordance with legend, he is depicted in chains. It is the only such stone in England, and only one other is known to survive in Europe. The church includes the family chapels of the Whartons and Musgraves.

Leaving Kirkby Stephen the rows of houses built by the Midland for its employees can be seen on each side of the line beside the A685 road which the line crosses. Curving round to the west, the line crosses Scandal Beck by the 12-arch Smardale Viaduct, which has the distinction of being the highest on the Midland, at 39 m (130 ft). The foundations for the 60,000 tons of grey limestone and millstone grit used in the viaduct had to be sunk 14 m (45 ft) below the river. When the viaduct was finished after 4^1/$_2$ years' work, the contractors asked the wife of John Crossley to lay the last stone; it bears the inscription 'This last stone was laid by Agnes Crossley, June 8th, 1875.' Midland passengers would often have seen a goods train on the Kirkby Stephen to Tebay line that once passed beneath the viaduct; the route carried prodigious quantities of coke from County Durham to the blast furnaces of west Cumberland, while finished products such as pig iron, rails and girders travelled the other way.

The short Crosby Garrett Tunnel is soon followed by the six-arch viaduct that dominates the village. For some reason the station here had a particularly

In conditions that attract scores of photographers, Midland Compound No. 1000 and LMS Jubilee 4-6-0 No. 5690 Leander head south over Smardale Viaduct in 1983. The 12-span structure is the second longest on the line after Ribblehead and once crossed over the North Eastern Railway's line from Darlington to Tebay.

A northbound train behind Class 45 No. 45143 crosses Smardale Viaduct. The viaduct crosses Scandal Beck which joins the River Eden to the east of Soulby.

long platform; it was more likely to assist in the loading of milk, since the station closed to passengers as early as 1952 through lack of patronage. A signalman at Crosby Garrett was largely responsible for a mishap to an excursion train returning from Edinburgh to Rochdale on a July night in 1888. Although the train was booked to be shunted into a siding at either Kirkby Stephen or Mallerstang to allow a Scotch express to overtake it, a decision was taken to shunt the excursion out of the way at Crosby Garrett, at 01.04. The 19-coach excursion was considerably longer than a normal passenger train, but the two guards did not inform the signalman of the fact, and the signalman never thought to ask. Although the train was too long for the siding, the accident would not have happened were it not for muddled signals and actions by the two guards and a railway inspector from Rochdale. The upshot was that the train rammed the buffer stops, injuring seven passengers and the inspector.

The station at Crosby Garrett was one of the few on the S&C that was perfectly sited for accessibility. The few houses cluster round the piers of the

Class 47 No. 47077 crosses Crosby Garrett Viaduct with a northbound train. The station closed in 1952, despite being well sited for the small community.

viaduct, from which can be seen, built on a steep hill for defensive reasons, the Church of St. Andrew. It is thought to be Anglo-Saxon in origin though the greater part of the building dates from an enlargement around 1175, and the projecting bell-turret on the west front was probably added in the thirteenth century. Cairns are to found on several of the surrounding hills.

The countryside is now much more open, with views to the west as far as the Lake District peaks. The rich pasture speaks of the milk traffic that was once a good source of revenue for the railway. Two miles north of Crosby Garrett the line crosses Griseburn Viaduct of seven arches. The viaduct piers are built of stone, but the arches were formed of bricks made on the site. A little further to the north is the site of Griseburn Ballast Sidings, where the signal box closed in 1981. The sidings were the scene of an unusual incident one November night in 1948, when work had finished re-railing some wagons

using a 50-ton breakdown crane. The crane was standing on the northbound line, on the 1 in 100 gradient, when it was nudged by the locomotive to which it was about to be coupled. The crane brakes had not been properly applied, and the crane began to descend the gradient. Sadly a railwayman was killed in the futile attempt to stop the heavy crane, which ran on, 'right line', as far as Lazonby, 23 miles away.

From Griseburn the Helm Beck is in view to the right, forming a very attractive stretch of line down to Helm Tunnel, the name being given to the

Right: With a train of typical length for the time, Class 45/1 No. 45108 crosses Crosby Garrett Viaduct with the 16.37 Leeds–Carlisle train on 29 June 1983. Below: Class 47 No. 47475 heads a train for Leeds through the site of Crosby Garrett station in 1990. Considerable quantities of milk were once loaded here.

Class 47 No. 47634 Henry Ford leaves the south portal of Helm Tunnel between Crosby Garrett and Ormside. A grocer from Carlisle opened a store to supply the navvies living in a camp near the tunnel, where the contractor provided a reading-room, coffee-house and hospital.

Opposite: LMS Jubilee 4-6-0 No. 45596 Bahamas heads a Carlisle-Oxenhope special near Ormside in 1992. The last Jubilees to operate expresses over the S&C under British Ralways were well recorded, often by photographers who had spent hours cleaning the locomotives prior to leaving the locomotive depot.

wind which can blow with particular ferocity hereabouts. Crossing an embankment, the line passes the site of Ormside station, which is just over half way between Settle and Carlisle. The station closed in 1952, the signal box eight years later. It was here, in the small hours of an August night in 1876, that the very first accident on the S&C occurred. The Ormside signalman received warning from Crosby Garrett that a northbound goods train had split in two. At the same moment he was offered by the Appleby signalman a Carlisle to St. Pancras express. The Ormside signalman should have stopped the express and allowed the goods a clear run, warning the driver by a handlamp signal that his train was divided. Instead he decided to stop both trains, but when the express arrived first he made a second error in allowing it to proceed with caution. At that point the first part of the goods passed the locomotive of the express, but a moment later the second section caught up the leading wagons and collided. Some of the wagons derailed, catching the side of the passing carriages and injuring two passengers and a guard.

The village of Ormside is just to the east of the line. At the far end of the village close to the river and hall is the Church of St. James, which has an eleventh-century doorway and a tower obviously built for defence. Almost 200 years ago the richest known example of Anglo-Saxon metalwork was found in the churchyard; made in the ninth century, it is called the Ormside Bowl and can be seen in York Museum.

A little to the north the line crosses the now broad River Eden by the ten-arched Ormside Viaduct, the start of a rare section of rising gradient towards Appleby. There is a view west from the viaduct over a bend in the Eden, which flows north-west through Carlisle to join the Solway. Over to the right the remnants of the Darlington–Kirkby Stephen–Penrith line come into view as it swings in from Warcop and the army camp that the truncated branch served long after the rest of the line closed in 1962. The final approach to Appleby is marked on the east side of the line by a large dairy which opened in 1931 as the Express Dairy and was rail-connected. At first the glass-lined milk tanks bound for London were attached to an afternoon train, but as traffic built up, it became a special working with up to 27 tanks a day being dispatched. During the 1950s the factory turned over to cheese production.

Appleby–Carlisle

Once the county town of Westmorland, Appleby is built around a large loop in the River Eden and was granted a charter by Henry I on the same day as the privilege was bestowed on York. Its historic importance is reflected in a former population of 11,000; today it has 2,400. At its centre is a long rectangular market place known as Boroughgate, which is marked at its upper end by High Cross and by the castle which is clearly visible from the station above the rooftops.

Dominating the town, Appleby Castle was in being by 1120 but it is impossible to date precisely the start of work. In 1174 it fell to the invading Scots army of William the Lion. The oldest part is the twelfth-century, square-plan stone keep, topped by four turrets, though the sandstone curtain walls also date from that century. The Clifford family became its owners in the late thirteenth century, and Lady Anne Clifford restored the keep, which is larger than William I's White Tower at the Tower of London. The east range was rebuilt in 1686–8 by Lady Anne's son-in-law, the Earl of Thanet, using stone from Brough and Brougham castles.

Today the castle is open to visitors: besides the Norman keep and Great Hall with Clifford family portraits and the painting Lady Anne commissioned to commemorate her inheritance, it has become a home for rare farm animals, under the auspices of the Rare Breeds Survival Trust, and for a large collection of wildfowl, pheasants, poultry and owls. Collections of rare bicycles and Roman armour can also be seen. A little to the north of the castle, Lady Anne built St. Anne's Hospital, a tranquil though rather austere red sandstone row of almshouses built around a courtyard in 1651–3 in the upper part of the town; it still houses retired ladies. The exceptionally broad main street has a number of fine buildings, notably the Moot Hall of 1596, where the town council has met for centuries, and the White House of 1756 on which every window has an ogee head. Little has survived the destructive raids of the Scots – the town was almost completely burned down in 1388 – but the street plan remains medieval even if the town has a Georgian and Victorian appearance.

At the lower end of Boroughgate is Low Cross and the Church of St. Lawrence. The bottom of the church's tower dates from Norman times, but the nave is largely around 1300 with a fifteenth-century screen. Lady Anne Clifford's family chapel was built in 1654–5; she lies here alongside her mother in a vault beneath her tomb. The organ was brought from Carlisle Cathedral in 1684, replacing one destroyed during the Civil War. The church bells were rung on the day in 1866 when news arrived of the successful passage of the S&C Bill through the House of Commons.

To the north-west of the town is the grammar school where George Washington's brothers were pupils. Market day is Saturday, but the most famous market is held only once a year, in June, when people from all over the country come to trade at the Horse Fair or to compete in trotting races.

There is an attractive riverside walk south from Appleby on a footpath beside the west bank, passing under the railway at Ormside and crossing the river by a footbridge near Ormside church. The return takes a path on the east side of the railway before crossing it by a small bridge before the town is reached.

Appleby has always been one of the most important sources of traffic on the S&C, and between 1880 and 1903 even had a local service to Penrith, timed to connect with expresses from St. Pancras and operated by the North Eastern Railway over the spur to the Eden Valley line. Appleby has long been a major cattle centre, with weekly stock auctions, and was third (to Settle and Lazonby) in the amount of livestock traffic handled by S&C stations. Prize cattle were sometimes accorded the superior comfort of horseboxes in which to travel. The goods shed is now occupied by Appleby Heritage Centre.

With the three gables given to larger stations, Appleby is unusual in being built of brick. The main buildings are on the west side, convenient for the

In 1993 an enterprising service of special trains was laid on between Carlisle and Kirkby Stephen using BR Standard Class 4MT 2-6-4T No. 80080, which is seen here on Armathwaite curve. The combination of some of Britain's finest landscapes and steam traction has made the S&C the foremost route for such excursions.

town. A plaque on the station commemorates a sad day in May 1978 when the well-known railway photographer, the Rt. Rev. Eric Treacy, formerly Lord Bishop of Wakefield, collapsed and died while waiting to photograph a steam train. A memorial service was held in September at Appleby station, at which the plaque was unveiled.

The two platforms are connected by an ornate footbridge. Until 1973 there were two signal boxes; the current box, built in 1951 to replace a burnt-out predecessor, is to the north of the station. The water tower at the south end is a reconstruction for use by steam specials, brought into use in 1991 and partly paid for through fundraising by the local Round Table.

As the train leaves Appleby and heads for Long Marton, the peculiar shapes of Dufton and Knock pikes can be seen to the east. The line crosses the Trout Beck by a five-arch bridge just before the site of Long Marton station which closed in 1970. At one time an aerial ropeway brought to the goods yard buckets of barytes from a mine on the fells to the east, depositing the loads in a hopper for onward movement by rail.

To the west of the line lies Kirkby Thore where there was a Roman fort and marching camp named Bravoniacum. No station was built to serve Kirkby Thore, but the British Gypsum works to the north-west of the village generates traffic for the railway. The principal flow is trainloads of desulphogypsum from the power station at Drax in North Yorkshire, which produces this by-product as part of the desulphurization process. A ten-year contract for this rail movement was signed in 1993.

New Biggin station closed in 1970, and the station is now a house. Frederick Williams relates a story told him by an engineer on the S&C regarding the survey and acquisition of land in the district. During a preliminary survey, he encountered the local landowner, Mr Crackmanthorpe, who inquired what they were doing. On hearing the purpose of their work, and that the intention was to drive the railway through an oak wood that belonged to him, the landowner was indignant. Realizing the likely difficulty the gentleman might pose, the engineer wisely suggested a visit from the Midland's General Manager might be in order. James Allport and John Crossley called on Mr Crackmanthorpe and clearly won him over with the benefits the railway

Opposite: Pacific No. 46229 Duchess of Hamilton crosses Long Marton Viaduct.
Below: Class 47 No. 47119 enters Appleby with a diverted train for Weston, 1982.

would confer on the area. The next meeting between the junior engineer and the landowner was marked by greater cordiality, the latter stating that he had only one condition to make. 'It is that you spare me the largest and finest oak in my wood.' The engineer readily agreed. 'Do you know what I want it for?' continued the proprietor. 'No sir, but whatever you want it for, it shall be saved,' replied the engineer. 'Well,' said Mr Crackmanthorpe good naturedly, 'it's to hang you and all the engineers of the Midland Railway upon it, for daring to come here at all!'

A four-arched viaduct takes the railway across Crowdundle Beck, which used to mark the county boundary between Westmorland and Cumberland and flows on past the National Trust garden of Acorn Bank. This seventeenth-century, 1¹/₂-acre walled garden is noted for its display of daffodils and for its herb garden, which has the largest collection of culinary and medicinal plants in the north. The manor house itself is a Sue Ryder home and is open by arrangement.

The first level crossing on the S&C is encountered at Culgaith, another station closed in 1970, but the 1908 signal box stands at the south end of the former platforms. The station was the only one on the S&C with non-standard buildings, probably because it was not opened until 1880, four years after most of the others. The station survives as a residence and has a more domestic appearance than the standard stations, which are unmistakably railway buildings even if attractively designed. The station master here had to make do with a cottage just behind the platform instead of a substantial two-storey house. There was never a goods shed here, but a significant amount of milk was sent out by rail.

There was an accident a little to the north of the station in 1930, when a ballast train and a stopping train from Hellifield to Carlisle met head-on, due to a combination of unfortunate errors by three railwaymen. The driver of the passenger train was killed, and a passenger later died in hospital. The damage done to the passenger locomotive, Claughton 4-6-0 No. 5971 *Croxteth*, was severe enough to warrant a rebuild, and the result was the first of the Patriot class.

The tunnels of Culgaith (604 m/661 yd) through hard red marl and Waste Bank (149 m/164 yd) follow in quick succession before a section that offers delightful views to the west over the meandering Eden and its confluence with the River Eamont which flows from Ullswater to the south-west of Penrith. It was to take advantage of the S&C's proximity to Ullswater and Penrith that the Midland had the road improved between **Langwathby**, the next station, and Penrith. For some years horse-drawn charabancs operated from Langwathby station during the summer months, offering tours to Ullswater. The station was

Opposite: Southbound LNER A2 Pacific No. 60532 Blue Peter at New Biggin.
Below: LNER A3 Pacific No. 4472 Flying Scotsman leaves Culgaith Tunnel on 27 July 1983. The A3 is running with the tender from A4 No. 4498 Sir Nigel Gresley.

reopened in 1986, but the beautifully kept station is now occupied by the 'Brief Encounter' café/restaurant. At first following the older spelling of the village, Langwathby station was known as Longwathby for five months after it opened in May 1876.

Only 1¹/₂ miles north of Langwathby is the closed station of Little Salkeld, preceded by a seven-arch viaduct over Briggle Beck. At the south end of the station site, the railway crosses over the minor road that has been incorporated into Sustrans's Sea to Sea cycle route from Whitehaven/Workington–Sunderland/Newcastle. Near the bridge is Little Salkeld Watermill, an eighteenth-century cornmill powered by a pair of cast-iron overshot wheels. Milling stoneground organic flours, it is open to visitors.

For such a small station, Little Salkeld seems to have been rather prone to accidents, having been the scene of no less than three. Even more oddly, two of them involved the same locomotive. The first occurred in January 1918 when a northbound express hauled by Compound 4-4-0 No. 1010 ran into a huge landslide in Long Meg cutting, only minutes after a platelayer had walked through without anything being amiss. The slip had been brought on by a thaw. Seven passengers were killed.

The next accident, in July 1933, could certainly have been avoided, and was caused by a complete disregard for regulations on the part of a porter-signalman made grumpy by having his lunch interrupted. Little Salkeld was one of the few signal boxes on the S&C that was usually switched out; that is,

Opposite: LMS Princess Royal Pacific No. 46203 Princess Margaret Rose passes Keld, just north of Appleby, with a southbound Cumbrian Mountain Express in 1994.
Below: In British Railways days, trains for Long Meg sidings generated a healthy freight traffic. LMS 8F 2-8-0 No. 48090 is seen here passing Kirkby Stephen.

the signal boxes on either side were put in direct contact and the signals at Little Salkeld were pulled off for up and down lines. The box was opened only when a goods train had to pick up or drop off wagons.

Being a quiet station, Little Salkeld no longer had a station master, and the person in charge was porter-signalman Hannah. His supervisor, the station master at Langwathby, was unaware that Hannah was in the habit of taking his lunch at 12.30, an hour earlier than he should have done, in order to oblige his landlady who regarded a 13.30 lunch as unacceptable to her regime. While having his lunch, Hannah heard the whistle of a goods train he wasn't expecting. The driver informed Hannah that he had a wagon of coal to drop off. Having had to abandon his lunch, Hannah truculently stomped off to the signal box to superintend the various shunting movements. Inexplicably he did not check with the signalmen on either side what trains were in the vicinity, nor did he inform them that he was opening the box to allow the wagon to be shunted. By moving the points, the home signals were automatically placed at danger, but not the distant signals. As the goods engine was propelling three wagons over a crossover between up and down lines, a southbound express hauled by No. 1010 came tearing out of the cutting to the north; the distant signal had shown a clear road through the station and the driver was making speed for the climb to his first stop at Appleby. The Compound struck the goods engine tender and leading wagon and derailed to the left, while the carriages careered to the right and collided with the rest of the goods train. Despite extensive damage to the carriages, no passengers were killed – carriage design and construction had improved significantly since pre-war days. However, the poor driver of the goods train, who was on the point of retirement, was fatally injured.

The final mishap at Little Salkeld was in 1961, when a northbound goods was derailed just north of the station and came into collision with a southbound goods, blocking both lines.

A little to the north-east of the village is Long Meg and Her Daughters, the second largest stone 'circle' in England – it is actually oval in plan, measuring about 110 × 93 m/360 × 305 ft. Neolithic in origin, it is thought to have once had about 70 stones, but today 27 still stand to a height of up to 2.7 m (9 ft). These are the daughters; Meg is a square stone standing 3.65 m (12 ft) high about 18.3 m (60 ft) outside the circle.

Further picturesque views are to be had of the Eden just past Little Salkeld as the line passes through parkland. Considerable traffic was once generated for the railway by Long Meg gypsum mine and plaster works to the north of Little Salkeld; the gypsum was quarried from 1875 to 1895 when it became

Preserved LMS 8F 2-8-0 No. 48151 passes Lazonby & Kirkoswald with a southbound excursion for Leeds in 1988. The once busy goods shed and yard has been taken over by a thriving bakery.

necessary to mine it. After grinding, the material was dried in coal-fired pans to produce commercial plaster of Paris. The remains of the extensive sidings that served the works can still be seen to the right, just before the line curves to the left to cross the River Eden for the last time, by means of a sandstone seven-arch viaduct. This had to be built using a cofferdam to protect the foundations, so difficult was it to find a secure footing for the piers. The river marks the transition from limestone to sandstone.

The parkland surrounding the house of Eden Lacy to the east of the line forms a beautiful setting and prompted construction of an ornamental bridge for the then landowner, Colonel Sanderson. On the right just before Lazonby Tunnel (90 m/99 yd) were Lazonby ballast sidings, where the signal box was taken out of use as long ago as 1878–9.

The now reopened station at **Lazonby & Kirkoswald** is conveniently situated for the former village, but Kirkoswald is about a mile to the east across the river. The elegant brick bridge that carries the road over the water can be seen from the railway. Kirkoswald is a good example of the impact the coming of the railway could have on commercial activity in a country district: it has a fine market square at its centre, but the long-established livestock markets once held here were moved to the station with the opening of the S&C. It became one of the busiest goods stations on the line, dominated by livestock traffic which even eclipsed that at Appleby and Settle during the period from 1916 to 1922. Trainloads of sheep from northern Scotland were received, and on stock sale days as many as 55 wagons might be sent off. Such sales naturally brought many buyers in by train, and the importance of locally based dealers was reflected in the special stopping of the northbound Scotch express at 04.30 to allow dealers to reach St. Boswells for the stock sales in the Borders town.

There were other commodities, too: three coal merchants had premises in the yard, crates of rabbits were sent to the West Riding, and timber and potatoes dispatched – vanloads of potato sacks would be received. Salmon caught in the Eden were sent to London in special boxes – anglers were allowed to keep one fish, but any more had to be sold on. Many of the fishermen were well-to-do men from Leeds and Bradford who would be met off the train at Lazonby by local ghillies.

Both villages have fine though very different churches: the Church of St. Nicholas at Lazonby was built in 1863 to the design of Anthony Salvin; the

church of St. Oswald in Kirkoswald was begun in Norman times, built at the foot of the hill to mark the site of the saint's baptisms. The son of a king of Northumbria, Oswald defeated and killed in battle near Hexham the tyrannical British king, Cadwalla, and became king of Northumbria. Oswald himself was later killed in battle in 642. A spring rises under the nave, feeding the well by the west wall of the church. The church has a separate square tower put up in the nineteenth century.

The buildings of a religious college founded in 1523 to the north of St. Oswald were put up around a fourteenth-century pele tower by Thomas de Dacre and his wife Isabel de Greystoke. After its Dissolution in 1547, it was adapted to become a house and it has been the home of the Fetherstonhaugh family for about four centuries. Little survives of a moated castle built in the

early thirteenth century except a tower. It was burnt down by the Scots in 1314, but rebuilt. Its last occupant was Lord William Howard who sold much of the materials after he moved out in 1604.

The section between Lazonby and Cotehill is particularly attractive, and has been described by some writers as the prettiest part of the Eden Valley. For several miles the river runs through a densely wooded gorge to right, precipitous slopes of birch and bracken dropping down to the water far below. The best way to enjoy this outstanding stretch of river is to walk beside it

Opposite: LNER A4 Pacific No. 4498 Sir Nigel Gresley heads north past Baron Wood, one of the most scenic parts of the line, especially in autumn.
Below: Southbound LMS Pacific No. 46229 Duchess of Hamilton at Baron Wood.

Opposite: LMS Pacific No. 6201 Princess Elizabeth threads Baron Wood in 1987. Below right: LMS Jubilee class 4-6-0 No. 45697 Achilles heads a train of Mk I stock past Cumwhinton with a Scottish tours charter train in 1965.

between Lazonby and Armathwaite, the next station north. A leaflet devoted to the Eden Gorge is available from TICs. Not to be missed on the east bank are the ancient Nunnery Walks, created near the confluence of the Eden and Groglin rivers to help walkers admire the nearby waterfalls and 61 m- (200 ft-) high sandstone cliffs. At a bend where river and railway are in close proximity is a place on the east bank known as Samson's Cave. This was named after a railway navvy who was involved in a brawl that ended in his opponent's death. Samson hid in the cave but was found, taken to Carlisle and hanged.

As well as sandstone cuttings, two tunnels interrupt the view – Baron Wood No. 1 (189 m/207 yd) and No. 2 (229 m/251 yd) – but there are more panoramas along the river as the valley broadens out and over extensive coniferous plantations before Armathwaite Tunnel, the line's last, 1¹/₂ miles south of the station. Before reaching **Armathwaite**, the line crosses a curving nine-arch viaduct. Besides the station buildings, the goods shed and signal box stand, the latter having been closed as recently as 1983 and now externally restored by Friends of the Settle–Carlisle Line. The village is just to the east of the line, though invisible from it because it is set beside the river, well below the railway. The castle, a four-storey pele tower in a glorious position by the River Eden, was adapted into a country house after it was acquired by William Sanderson in 1712, the front being a typically northern style of Early Georgian.

The Chapel of Christ and Mary has stained glass in the east window designed by Morris & Co. in 1914, though long after the deaths of William Morris and Sir Edward Burne-Jones, who had designed many of the windows produced by the company. Also in the village is the Eden Valley Woollen Mill, which is open to visitors and produces a variety of woven fabrics that can be bought by the metre or made into garments.

During construction of the railway, the people of Armathwaite witnessed one of the relatively few incidents of public disorder caused by the navvies: an Irishman was killed in a fight, and there ensued a stand-off between a hundred English navvies and the armed constabulary.

Leaving Armathwaite, the railway again looks down on the Eden, from what is, surprisingly, one of the largest embankments on the railway, made up of 305,810 m³ (400,000 yd³) of material. The river snakes its way through the pastoral landscape between tree-lined banks, but the Gorge was the climax of the S&C's scenic delights, and the views from here onwards are pleasant, but

lack the scale and drama of what has gone before. The line crosses the seven-arch Dry Beck Viaduct before curving to the left to pass close to a now wooded place on the river called Eden Brows. The embankment here gave the builders great trouble, since tipping to form it merely caused the ground to slip into the river. Crossley ignored the sceptics who said that the terrain made construction of a railway an impossibility and succeeded in building the line across the slope; he did this by sinking vertical shafts that were filled with stone and thereby acted as both drains and supports to act against further slips. The embankment leads on to High Stand Gill Viaduct, which has four arches and crosses the wooded ravine that takes the stream down to the Eden.

The railway is taken over a minor road by one of the S&C's few level crossings, controlled by the oldest signal box on the line. Low House Crossing was opened in 1900, only a short distance south of Cotehill station. Closed in 1952, this station was for a short time called both High Stand Gill and

Knothill, the latter being the name of gypsum quarries and a plaster and cement works that were served by a short branch from a point directly opposite Cotehill signal box, which was also closed in 1952. Little remains to mark the site of the station apart from a row of Midland cottages. The church of 1868 at Cotehill has a most curious north-east tower with a top shaped like a stupa.

The line veers away from the Eden and passes a group of derelict sidings, but still with operating signal box. Howe & Co's Siding (actually there were numerous sidings here) dates back to the opening of the S&C, although the present box replaced the original one in 1916. A branch went off to the south-west to serve a tile works, a plaster works and several brickworks. Howe & Co.'s Siding is the 'fringe' box to Carlisle Power Signal Box and marks the end of mechanical signalling, replaced by electric colour light signals into Carlisle.

Below: Carlisle station, before the railway companies were amalgamated in 1922, was one of the most interesting places to watch trains, with the colourful liveries of eight different railways to be seen. The Midland was the latecomer, but S&C traffic compelled enlargement; although the MR was denied a place on the LNWR and CR Joint Committee which ran the station.

NBR J36 0-6-0 No. 673 Maude passes London Road Junction, Carlisle, on 17 May 1980, en route to the 150th anniversary celebrations of the Liverpool & Manchester.

A mile or so further north are the remains of Cumwhinton station, which was closed in 1956. It was near the station that a wolf was run over by an express in December 1904; the animal had escaped from private grounds in Allendale to the east of Alston and had killed about 40 sheep during its days of freedom.

Less remains of Scotby station, which was the first station on the S&C to be closed, in 1942, and the signal box was also an early economy, closing in 1909. As late as 1600 Scotby was the victim of one of the cross-border raids that had been going on for centuries; under the joint command of the Border reiver Kinmont Willie, a 140-strong band of outlaws known as Sandy's Bairns burnt and pillaged, taking prisoners and a hundred head of cattle. Now almost a suburb of Carlisle, Scotby has a church of 1854 built by Anthony Salvin.

The line from Newcastle appears to the north, and the two meet at Petteril Bridge Junction. Before the junction, the land on either side of the line was once occupied by extensive goods and carriage sidings and (on the left) by Durran Hill engine shed. This could accommodate 24 engines around a 17 m (55 ft) turntable. The shed was closed in 1936 but reopened during the Second World War and finally closed as late as 1959. The goods yard and attractive goods shed to the north of the railway after Petteril Bridge belonged to the North Eastern Railway, which owned the railway from Newcastle.

The final approach to **Carlisle** Citadel station entails a sharp curve to the right to join the West Coast main line at the south end of the station. Its imposing façade incorporating a clock-tower was designed by Sir William Tite in the late 1840s, long before the Midland arrived, using a Tudor-Gothic style to harmonize with the crenellated Citadel law courts to the left outside the station. These were designed by Sir Robert Smirke and completed in 1810–11.

Following the opening of the S&C, it was quickly apparent that Carlisle station could not cope with the trains of seven companies travelling over eight routes into the border town. Accordingly it was enlarged in 1878–81 to create new platforms and offices, covered by a ridge-and-furrow roof of almost 6 acres. The city had become one of Britain's foremost railway junctions, with more railway companies entering the city than any other city apart from the capital. Although all seven companies ran their passenger trains into Carlisle Citadel station, all had separate goods stations and most had their own engine sheds, some very large establishments. In addition, Cowan, Sheldon & Co.

Opposite: LNER A4 Pacific No. 4498 Sir Nigel Gresley at Carlisle Citadel station.

set up an engineering works in the city in 1847, becoming one of the foremost producers of railway cranes, many of which were exported all over the world.

Carlisle was founded by the Celts, and developed as Luguvalium by the Romans as a defensive base for Hadrian's Wall. There appear to have been two separate forts, and the town grew to cover about 28 ha (70 acres). Carlisle was captured from the Scots by William Rufus in 1092, when work on the castle was begun, creating a wooden palisaded enclosure on a bluff overlooking the Eden. Work began on the great tower in 1122 and was continued after the town surrendered to David I of Scotland in 1136; it was completed by 1174, when the town was besieged by William the Lion. The principal building of the castle, the tower has been greatly altered over the years – for example, it was modified during Henry VIII's reign to accept the use of heavy guns. Mary Queen of Scots was imprisoned there in 1568.

In 1292 fire destroyed most of the buildings in the city. Over four centuries later, the rebuilt city withstood a siege of nine months during the Civil War, eventually it was taken by a Scottish army in 1645. A century later Bonnie Prince Charlie proclaimed his father king at the market cross at one end of English Street, but within weeks the city had fallen to the bloody Duke of Cumberland.

The castle, open throughout the year, also played a major role in the long history of cross-border raiding and feuding, some of the culprits being interned in its dungeons. The 300-year-history of the county's regiment, the King's Own Royal Borderers, is housed in the castle, the regiment's home since 1873.

In the centre of the city is the timber-framed Guildhall built in 1407, now a museum. The cathedral is one of the smallest in England. It has its origins in a religious establishment that was sacked by the Danes around 860, but it is noted for the carving of the canopies to the choir-stalls, the complete and well-preserved series of symbols of each month – a tradition thousands of years old – which can be found on the capitals, and the dramatic stained glass in the east window which dates from the fourteenth century.

The city's award-winning museum and art gallery is at Tullie House, a Jacobean residence in Castle Street; it has an exhibition on the railways of the town and area, as well as a herb garden, a display covering the Romans and an exciting audio-visual display on the border reivers. It is also the national study centre for the whole of Hadrian's Wall. Thanks largely to the bequest of the playwright and poet Gordon Bottomley, who died in 1948, the gallery includes works by Ford Maddox Brown, Edward Burne-Jones, Paul Nash, Samuel Palmer and Rossetti, as well as acquisitions of works by Lowry, Pissarro, Sickert and Stanley Spencer.

Index

Page numbers in *italics* denote references to illustrations.

A

accidents;
Ais Gill 1913, 63–64, *64*, 67
Ais Gill 1947, 63
Blea Moor 1952, 49
Blea Moor Tunnel 1878, 51
Crosby Garrett 1888, *73*
Culgaith 1930, 83
Garsdale Water Troughs, 55
Griseburn-Lazonby 1948, 74
Hawes Junction *now Garsdale* 1891, 58
Hawes Junction *now Garsdale* 1910, *26*, 58–60, 63
Little Salkeld 1918, 85
Little Salkeld 1933, 85–86
Little Salkeld 1961, 86
Ormside 1876, 76
Settle Junction 1878, 40
Settle Station 1960, 41, *43*
Stainforth 1961, 43
Ais Gill, 7, *13*, *18*, *28*, *31*, 48, 60, 63, *63*, 64, *66*, 67
Allport, Sir James, 8, 9, 14, 80, 83
Appleby, 22, 25, 26, 28, 36, 76, 79–80, *80*, 86
architecture, 22
Armathwaite, 22, 36, 78, 91
Arten Gill Viaduct, *20*, 51, *53*
Ashwell, William H., 48

B

Baron Wood, *88*, *89*, *90*, 91
Batty Green, 47
Batty Moss, 20, 22, 47
Baugh Fell, 55
Beeching report, 35
Bell Busk, 40
Birkbeck, George, 40
Birkett, *32*, 67, *68*, *69*
Blea Moor, 40, 48–49, *52*
Blea Moor Tunnel, 16, 40, 47, 49, *50*, 51, *51*
Bonnie Prince Charlie, 95
Bottomley, Gordon, 95
Bowling Green Mill, 39
Briggle Beck, 85

C

Carlisle, 10, 12, 28, *33*, 36, *37*, 52, 76, 92, *92*, *93*, *94*, 95
Caudle, Samuel, 64, 67
Chapel-le-Dale, 20, 47

Churches;
Appleby, St. Lawrence, 79
Armathwaite, Chapel of Christ and Mary, 91
Carlisle Cathedral, 95
Chapel-le-Dale, 20, 47
Cotehill, 92
Crosby Garrett, St. Andrew, 74
Dent, St. Andrew, 55
Horton, St. Oswald, 43
Kirkby Stephen, 67, 71
Kirkoswald, St. Oswald, 88
Lazonby, St. Nicholas, 86
Ormside, St. James, 76
Scotby, 95
Settle (plaque), *17*
Clifford, Lady Anne, 39, 67, 79
closure proposals and notices, 25–26, 37, 47
Clough, River, 55
Coal Road, 52
Condor container service, 28
conservation area, 22
construction, 12, 14–20, 47, *see also* navvies;
Blea Moor tunnel, 49, 51
costs, 10, 12, 20, 49, 51
Eden Brows embankment, 91
Ribblehead Viaduct, 48
Rise Hill tunnel, 55
Smardale Viaduct, 71
Cotehill, 91
Cotton, Ron, 37
Cowan, Sheldon & Co., 95
Crackmanthorpe, Mr, 80, 83
Craven Lime Company, 43
Crosby Garrett, 22, 71, 73–74, *73*, *74*, *75*
Crossley, Agnes, 71
Crossley, John Sidney, 8, 10, 12, 14, 16, 17, 19–20, 22, 67, 80, 83, 91
Crowdundle, 83
Culgaith, 22, 83, *83*
Cumbria County Council, 37
Cumbrian Mountain Express, 36, *38*, *43*, 56, *62*, *68*, *84*
Cumbrian Mountain Pullman, *83*
Cumwhinton, *91*, 95

D

Dales Rail services, 36, 37
Dandry Mire Viaduct, 60, 61, 67
Defence, Ministry of, 29, 57
Dent, 22, *33*, 36, 48, 51–52, *54*, 55
Dent Head, 16, 51

Dentdale, 6, 51
desulphogypsum, 29, 80
diesel multiple unit class 1 56, *59*
Drax, 29, 80
Dry Beck Viaduct, 91
Durran Hill engine shed, 67, 95

E

Eamont, River, 83
Eden Brows, 91
Eden Gorge, 91
Eden Lacy, 86
Eden, River and Valley, 17, 22, 67, 76, 83, 86, 88, 91
Edinburgh, 10, 24
Elgar, Sir Edward, 40
engine changes, 30
English, Welsh and Scottish Railways, 29
Ethel generator units, *51*

F

Five Rise Locks, 39
Follows, George, 64, 67
freight traffic, 28–29, *28*, *29*, 35, 43, *66*, 85, 86 *see also* types of traffic
Friends of the Settle-Carlisle line, 22, 37, 43, 45, 91

G

gangers' hut, *17*
Gargrave, 40
Garsdale, 6, 22, 27, 36, 52, 55, *55*, 57–60, *58*, *59*, *60*
Giggleswick, 40
Glasgow, 24, 28, 36
Glasgow and South Western Railway, 12, 24
goods sheds, 22
Great Knoutberry Hill, 51
Great Northern Railway, 10
Great Pennine Fault, 67
Griseburn, 63, 74
Grisedale Crossing, 63
Groglin, River, 91
gypsum quarries and works, 80, 86, 92

H

Hangman's Bridge, *29*
Hannah, Porter, 86
Hawes Junction, 57 *see also* Garsdale
Hellifield, *22*, *23*, 28, *33*, 39, *40*
Helm, 74, 76, 76
Helwith Bridge, 43
High Stand Gill *later Cotehill*, 91–92
Horton Lime works, 43
Horton-in-Ribblesdale, 36, 43, 45, 48
Howe & Co.'s Sidings, 92
Hudson, George, 8

I

inclined plane railway, 43
Ingleborough, 6, 43, 45
Ingleton, 40
Inverness, 24
Iron Age fort, 43

J

jet engine tests, 34, *34*

K

Keighley, 39, *58*
Keighley and Worth Valley Railway, 39, 58
Keld, *84*
Kilsby Tunnel, *16*
King's Own Royal Borderers, 95
Kinmont Willie, 95
Kirkby Stephen, 20, 22, 36, 43, 55, 67, 68, 71, *85*
Kirkby Thore, 80
Kirkoswald, 86
knitting industry, 55
Knock pike, 80
Knothill station *later Cotehill*, 92

L

Lancashire and Yorkshire Railway, 12, 39
Lancaster and Carlisle Railway, 10, 12
landscape and views, 6, 20, 45, 51, 55, 83, 86, 88, 91
Langwathby, 36, 83, 85
Lazonby, 28, 36, 55, 74, 86, 91
Lazony and Kirkoswald station, 86, *87*
Leeds, 24, 25, 26, 37, 39
Leeds and Liverpool Canal, 39, 40
Leicester, 30
level crossings, 83, 91
Little Salkeld, 85–86
livestock traffic, 28, 79, 86
locomotives, 30–32;
0-6-0 LMSR classes, *19*, 32
0-6-0 NBR J36 class, *93*
2-6-0 LMSR Crab class, 28, 32
2-6-4T BR 4MT class, *78*
2-8-0 LMSR 8F class & WD and 2-10-0 9F class, 32, 85, 87
4-4-0 MR & LMSR classes, 30, *30*, *31*, *32*, *70*
4-6-0 LMSR class 5 Black fives, 32, 44, 54, 55
4-6-0 LMSR Jubilee class, *13*, *31*, 32, 40, 55, 70, 77, 91
4-6-0 LMSR Royal Scot class, *11*, *25*, 32
4-6-0 SR *Lord Nelson*, 53

4-6-2 BR *Duchess of Gloucester*, 41
4-6-2 LMSR *Duchess of Hamilton*, 27, 35, *38*, *62*, *81*, *88*
4-6-2 LMSR *Princess Elizabeth*, 90
4-6-2 LMSR *Princess Margaret Rose*, 61, 65, 84
4-6-2 LNER A2 class *Blue Peter*, 82
4-6-2 LNER A3 class *Flying Scotsman*, 7, *18*, 50, 60, 83
4-6-2 LNER A4 class *Golden Eagle*, 49
4-6-2 LNER A4 class *Mallard*, 69
4-6-2 LNER A4 class *Sir Nigel Gresley*, 45, 46, 56, 89, *94*
4-6-2 LNER A4 class *Union of South Africa*, 68
4-6-2 SR Pacific classes, 43, 51
diesel class 31, 32
diesel class 37, 52
diesel class 45, 72, 75
diesel class 47, *20*, 42, 48, 58, 66, 73, 74, 76
diesel class 60, 29
trials, 32
Loki, 71
London and North Western Railway, 10, 12, 24, 32
London, Midland and Scottish Railway, 25
Long Drag, the, *33*
Long Marton, 80, *81*
Long Meg and Her Daughters, 86
Long Meg Cutting and Sidings, 85, *85*
Low Gill, 10
Low House Level Crossing, 91
Lunds Viaduct, 60, *62*

M

Mallerstang, 63–64, *65*, 67
map of line, 37
meal stops, 24
Metcalf, James, 64, 67
Midland Gothic style, 22
Midland Railway, 8–9, 10, 12, 30, 63
Midland Railway coaches, 9, 24, *24*, 26, 60, 67
Midland Railway heraldic device, *12*
Midland Railway (Settle to Carlisle) Act, 12
milk traffic, 28, 74, 76, 83
mineral traffic, 28–29, 43, 71, 80
Moorcock, 60, *61*, *62*, 67
Mossdale Moor pits, 52

Moughton Fell, 43
Musgrave family, 67, 71

N

navvies, *16*, 17, *17*, 19–20, 47, 55, 67, 76, 91
New Biggin, 16, 80, *82*
Nicholson, William, 63–64, 67
Nixon's Quarries, 51
Normanton, 24, 30
North British Railway, 10, 12, 24, 25
North Eastern Railway, 10, 57, 71, 79, 95
North of England Union Railway, 10, 16
Northallerton, 57
Nottingham, 36
Nunnery Walks, 91

O

October Luke Fair, 71
operation of line, 33–34
origins of line, 10
Ormside, 76, 77, 79
Oswald, King, 88

P

passenger services, 24–26
Pendragon Castle, 67
Penine Way, 43
Penyghent, 6, 43
Petteril Bridge, 16, 95
Pig Yard Museum, 40
Preston's Folly, 40

R

railway cranes, 95
Railway Heritage Trust, 39, 45
railway manias, 10, 20
Rare Breeds Survival Trust, 79
Redmire, 57
Ribble, River, 43
Ribblehead, 33, *35*, 36, 45, 47
Ribblehead Viaduct, *14*, *15*, 36, *36*, 37, *46*, 47, 48–49, *48*, *49*
Ribblesdale, 6, 22
Ribblesdale Lime Co., 43
Rise Hill, 51, 55
Roman camp and forts, 80, 95

S

Salt Lake Cottages, 45
Salt, Sir Titus, 39
Saltaire, 39
Salvin, Anthony, 86, 95
Samson's Cave, 91
Sanders, I. H., 22
Scandel Beck, 71, 72
Scotby, 25, 95
Scotch expresses, 24
Sedburgh, 52
Sedgwick, Adam, 55

Selside, *44*, 45, *45*
Settle, 22, 25, 26, 40, 86
Settle Junction, 16, 39, 40, Settle–Carlisle Joint Action Committee, 37
Sherrif Brow Bridge, *42*
Shotlock Hill, *56*, 63
Skipton, *19*, 30, 36, 39
small engine policy, 30
Smardale, 16, 70, 71, 72
snowploughs, *19*, *33* see also weather
soil conditions, 20, 67
South House Moor, 45
Stainforth, *38*, 42, 43, *43*
station buildings, 22 *see also* individual stations
station closures, 25–26
station gardens, 37
station re-openings, 36
Stranraer, 24
strip lynchets, 68
St. Anne's Hospital, 79
St. Boswells, 57
St. Pancras Station and Hotel, *9*, 24
Sustran's sea-to-sea cycle route, 85
Sutherland, Signalman, 64, 67
Sutton, Alfred, 58–60

T

Thames–Clyde Express, 24, *25*, 49, *84*
Thames–Forth Express, 24–25
Thames–Tyne Express, 27
Three Peaks, 6, 43
Tiplady, James, 20
Tommy Road, 67
Trainload Freight, 29
Transrail, 29
Treacy, Eric, 80
Trout Beck, 80
Tullie House, 95
Tunnels, 14;
Armathwaite, 91
Baron Wood, *88*, *89*, *90*, 91
Birkett, *32*, 67, 68
Blea Moor, 16, 40, 47, 49, *50*, 51, *51*
Crosby Garrett, 71
Culgaith, 83, *83*
Helm, 74, 76, *76*
Kilsby, *16*
Lazonby, 86
Moorcock, 60, *62*
Rise Hill, 51, 55
Shotlock Hill, *56*, 63
Waste Bank, 83
turntable at Garsdale, 58, *58*

U

Ullswater, 83
unstaffed stations, 45

V

Viaducts, 14;
Ais Gill, *29*, *66*, 67
Armathwaite, 91
Arten Gill, *20*, 51, *53*
Briggle Beck, 85
Crosby Garrett, 71, *73*, *75*
Crowdundle, 83
Dandry Mire, 60, *61*, 67
Dent Head, 51
Dry Beck, 91
Griseburn, 74
High Stand Gill, 91
Lunds, 60, *62*
Moorcock, 60, *61*, 67
Ormside, 76
Ribblehead, *14*, *15*, 36, *36*, 37, *46*, 47, 48–49, *48*, *49*
Smardale, 70, 71, 72

W

Wainwright's coast-to-coast walk, 71
Warcop, 76
Waste Bank, 83
water troughs, 55, *55*
Waverley route, 10, 25
Waverley, The, *11*, 25
weather;
1947, *33*, 34, *34*, 52, 63
1963, 52, *54*
during construction, 20
jet engine tests, 34, *34*
reporting, 47
snow and ice, 33–34, *33*, 34, 51–52, *54*, 63
snowplough, *19*
water troughs, 55
wind, *33*, 47, 49, 58, 76
Wensleydale line, 57
West Coast main line, 10, 24, 25, 26, 35, 95
Wharton family and portrait, 67–68, 71
Whernside, 6, 43, 51
Wild Boar Fell, 7, 67
Winskill Scar, 43
World War I, 25, 28
World War II, 25, 28, 32, 95

Y

Yorkshire Dales National Park, 6, 22, 36, 37, 43, 45

Index compiled by
Ian D. Crane